It's All About the Numbers

Teaching Christians How to Reach the Lost With Results

RILEY STEPHENSON

KENNETH COPELAND PUBLICATIONS

It's All About the Numbers
Teaching Christians How to Reach the Lost With Results

ISBN 978-1-60463-214-9   30-0824

18 17 16 15 14 13   7 6 5 4 3 2

Kenneth Copeland Publications
Fort Worth, TX 76192-0001

For more information about Kenneth Copeland Ministries, visit kcm.org or call 1-800-600-7395 (U.S. only) or +1-817-852-6000.

Contents

Introduction

You were born to go! You were born to reach your world for Jesus Christ! Forget about any previous ideas or traditions you have had concerning the subject of evangelism. I want to show you a more excellent way in reaching the lost—the way of love (see 1 Corinthians 12:31). I want to teach you what the Lord has taught me in witnessing to others. I pray this book will inspire you to go the distance and change someone's eternal destiny.

*The fruit of the righteous
is a tree of life; and he that
winneth souls is wise.*

Proverbs 11:30

*And they that be wise shall shine
as the brightness of the firmament;
and they that turn many to
righteousness
as the stars for ever and ever.*

Daniel 12:3

Passion for Souls

I have a confession to make! I hope you are sitting down. If not, grab a chair. This may shock some of you. Are you ready? Here it comes! Yes, I must confess, I'm "in it" for the numbers! I want to see people by the millions come to Jesus before He returns! I want to see numbers of people from every race, every religion, and every area on this planet saved! It is God's will that all men be saved!

You know, let's all be honest with one another. We're all "in it" for the numbers. It just depends on what your "it" is. Your "it" might be your job. At the end of the week when you get your paycheck, "the numbers" reflect the hours you've worked! If you are an accountant, you are definitely in it for the numbers. If you work for the IRS, you're in it for the numbers! Think about someone who is on a strict diet. Their "it" is calories or pounds. They count how many calories they can have, and they definitely count how many pounds they have lost! A runner counts how many miles he has run.

A businessman will let you know how many years he has been in business. Some businesses advertise the date established right on the sign so you can see how many "numbers" of years they've been in business. This usually gives them more credibility. A good businessman will set a goal every year as to how much money he wants to make by the end of the year.

What about churches? They do the same thing. They "record" attendance. They plan annual budgets for programs based on the "numbers." Also, a church will evaluate the success of a meeting based on the numbers. Let's face it: Numbers are important to God!

In John 21:11, the Bible says Peter caught 153 fish! God thought "numbers" so important, He recorded the number of fish caught on that day. Let's not get all spiritual when we set a "number of souls" goal. God's desire is that people come to Jesus by the thousands! We desire to see all of our family, friends, co-workers and acquaintances pulled out of the flames of hell (see Jude 23)!

One of my favorite quotes is, "We count people because people count." Christians have said to me, "Now brother, you shouldn't count the number of people saved. You shouldn't make it look like you're putting another notch on your gospel belt." Thank you for saying that! I want my "gospel belt" so notched up with souls that have given their lives to Jesus that you can't even tell it's a gospel belt! Did you know that God is in it for the numbers? Yes, He wrote a book in the Bible called Numbers!

My goal is to see as many "numbers" of people go to heaven as I possibly can! This goal has been the driving force of my ministry. You see, people who don't share this same dream assume I am only in it for the numbers. And you know what? They are right!

I attended a meeting several years ago where Gloria Copeland was preaching on seeking God's way of doing things from Matthew 6:33. She made the statement, "The only thing you do in life that will matter when you die is what you've done for Jesus." If I had gone to be with the Lord at that moment, not much would have mattered.

Several years later I was meditating on Matthew 6:33, and the Lord reminded me of a message I had heard preached. The Lord told me to combine Matthew 6:33 with Luke 19:10 from *The Amplified Bible*. This is what it says: "But *seek* (aim at and strive after) first of all His kingdom, His righteousness, *His way of seeking and saving that which was lost*, and then all these things taken together will be given you besides."

The Lord wants us to seek after the lost like a hunter seeks his game! A hunter sets the crosshairs on his scope to line up with the target. There is so much preparation before a hunt. A real hunter prepares for the hunt. I have a friend who is a serious hunter. Before he hunts, he sights in his rifle at 100 yards, 200 yards, 300 yards and up to 500 yards! He goes out and buys all the equipment he needs to make his hunt a big success.

God wants us to set our sights on souls! Target in on sharing the one thing that pulled you out of the empty life you were living. You were on an endless road going nowhere when someone talked to you. Someone invited you to church; maybe it was a co-worker. Or someone handed you a gospel tract. Let's never forget the time we got saved!

What is your salvation testimony? Obviously the person got results in one way or another who shared or led you to the Lord! I'm so glad you know Jesus! If you do not know Jesus, turn your life over to Him now. Turn to page 45 and pray the salvation prayer.

I will never forget the people through the years who witnessed to me before I got saved. I thank God for those people. I thank God they were not afraid to share Jesus with me. I really believe if we get involved in "His way" of seeking and saving the lost, God will get in our business and see that our needs are met!

Jesus said, "Look around you! Vast fields are ripening all around us and are ready now for the harvest" (see John 4:35). They are ready! They are ready! They are ready! Say this out loud: "They are ready!"

Right now, you and I could go to a mall or grocery store and tell people the good news. And according to the Bible, they are ready; so if they are ready, they will get saved! You don't need to wait any longer! They are ready! Jesus is saying the same thing today! He doesn't change. The only thing that has changed is that more than 2,000 years have passed. How much more ready are the people now!

*Everyone is sent. Jesus sent all
believers into the earth....
We're all told to evangelize. We're
all supposed to share Jesus.
"Go into all the world.
Preach the gospel."
That's to every believer.*

—Terri Copeland Pearsons

*But seek (aim at and strive after)
first of all His kingdom and His
righteousness (His way of seeking
and saving that which was lost), and
then all these things taken together
will be given you besides.*

Matthew 6:33 & Luke 19:10, *AMP*

CHAPTER 2

What Is Evangelism?

What is evangelism? Before I tell you what it is, let me show you what it is not. It is not grabbing the biggest Bible you can find, setting up a platform on the corner of the busiest intersection in town, and shouting at people, telling them they are going to hell. It is not holding a religious debate with someone of another religion and quoting hundreds of scriptures. It is not telling another denomination, "You're wrong and I'm right." No, the term evangelism comes from the Greek word *euangelizo,* which means "to announce the good news." Telling someone, "You're going to hell" is not announcing the good news!

We have been evangelistic about many things without realizing it. For example, when there's a sale on ties at a local department store, I tell others. When I eat a good steak at a local restaurant, I tell others. When I see a good movie, I will call and tell my friends. We talk about these things on our lunch break, or in passing, or as "ice breakers" to people we don't even know!

Ladies, you know you're evangelistic! I've heard the following from ladies: "Susie, have you heard about that designer dress on sale at the department store? They are having a 50-percent-off sale, girl! You'd better get over there!" Well, in the same way we are evangelistic about the things we enjoy in life, let's get busy telling others that God loves them and He's not holding anything against them (see 2 Corinthians 5:17-21).

Think about how good you feel when you save your friend some money on the tie that was on sale, or when he takes his family out to that great steak house. Think about how good you feel when you save your friend several dollars by telling her about the half-price designer dress. How much more wonderful you will feel when you share your testimony with someone and through that testimony he gives his life to Jesus Christ! God is in the people business! People are His No. 1 priority! God cares about the lost—so should we!

It is interesting to note that people who are lost know they are lost. When I ask people where they would go if they died that day, two-thirds of the people say they would go to hell. A large percentage of people say they would go to heaven because they are good or go to church. I heard a preacher say one time that going to McDonald's will not make you a hamburger any more than going to church will make you a Christian.

Brother and Sister, I want you to know there will be church members in hell! There will be pastors in hell! You may say, "Brother Riley, how can you say that?" I'm glad you asked! Let me show you from the Word of God what Jesus said about those who enter into the kingdom of heaven.

Look at Matthew 7:21-23:

> Not every one that saith unto me, Lord, Lord, shall
> enter into the kingdom of heaven; but he that doeth
> the will of my Father which is in heaven. Many will say
> to me in that day, Lord, Lord, have we not prophesied

in thy name? and in thy name have cast out devils?
and in thy name done many wonderful works? And
then will I profess unto them, I never knew you: depart
from me, ye that work iniquity.

You will find there are people who *know* God and there are people who *know about* God. It is important we get the good news of what Jesus has done out to the people. Simply put, evangelism is love in action; it is sharing the same good news someone shared with you! Love gives and never gives up! Love leads people to Jesus! *You* can lead people to Jesus!

For God sent not his Son into the world to condemn the world; but that the world through him might be saved.

John 3:17

CHAPTER 3

Don't Hide
Among the
Baggage

The children of Israel wanted a king so badly that the Lord anointed Saul to be king over Israel. Saul was anointed to be king and Israel needed him, yet he was hiding among the baggage. Let's read about this in 1 Samuel 10:21-22 *(AMP):*

> When he had caused the tribe of Benjamin to come near by their families, the family of Matri was taken. And Saul son of Kish was taken. But when they looked for him, *he could not be found.* Therefore they inquired of the Lord further, if the man would yet come back. And the Lord answered, Behold, *he has hidden himself among the baggage.*

Matthew 9:38 says, "Pray ye therefore the Lord of the harvest, that he will send forth labourers into his harvest." I believe God is looking for people to go out and be a witness for Him but they can't be found. He can't get them to go because they have hidden themselves among the baggage.

Say this aloud: "God, You can use me! I will not hide myself among the baggage!"

We can become so wrapped up in the circumstances and situations of life, we lose sight of the real reason Jesus came—which is explained in Luke 19:10. Our adversary, the devil, tries to distract us from the Great Commission. We have to see these distractions for what they are. Ephesians 6:12 reminds us that we wrestle not against flesh and blood but against principalities, powers, rulers of the darkness of the world, and spiritual wickedness in high places. Our battle is a spiritual battle.

We have a good description by Jesus of what happened to Saul that caused him to run and hide among the baggage.

> The farmer plants the Word. Some people are like the seed that falls on the hardened soil of the road. No sooner do they hear the Word than Satan snatches away what has been planted in them. And some are like the seed that lands in the gravel. When they first hear the Word, they respond with great enthusiasm. But there is such shallow soil of character that when the emotions wear off and some difficulty arrives, there is nothing to show for it. The seed cast in the weeds represents the ones who hear the kingdom news but are overwhelmed with worries about all the things they have to do and all the things they want to get. The stress strangles what they heard, and nothing comes of it. But the seed planted in the good earth represents those who hear the Word, embrace it, and produce a harvest beyond their wildest dreams (Mark 4:14-20, *MSG*).

If you look back at 1 Samuel 9:27, you see that Saul was told to hear the Word of God. I believe this is what happened. Saul heard the Word of God. Faith came as a result (see Romans 10:17). Saul had great enthusiasm. Samuel anointed him. Then I believe Saul started understanding what being the king of Israel meant. He became overwhelmed with the worry of all the kingly things he had to do and all the kingly things he needed to get. The stress he was under strangled the Word and nothing came of it.

Let's look at a New Testament example of this.

> While all this was going on, Peter was down in the courtyard. One of the Chief Priest's servant girls came in and, seeing Peter warming himself there, looked hard at him and said, "You were with the Nazarene, Jesus." He denied it: "I don't know what you're talking about." He went out on the porch. A rooster crowed. The girl spotted him and began telling the people standing around, "He's one of them." He denied it again. After a little while, the bystanders brought it up again. "You've got to be one of them. You've got 'Galilean' written all over you." Now Peter got really nervous and swore, "I never laid eyes on this man you're talking about." Just then the rooster crowed a second time. Peter remembered how Jesus had said, "Before a rooster crows twice, you'll deny me three times." He collapsed in tears (Mark 14:66-72, *MSG*).

Peter was with "The Word" for three years. He ate, drank, slept, traveled, and even ministered with "The Word." I used to be like Peter. I had a job in a factory; I worked there for years never sharing my faith. When someone would make a comment about "those holy rollers" or television evangelists, I would walk off fearing what my co-workers would think if they found out I was one of those holy rollers. What was I doing? I was being like Peter and Saul in that I was denying Jesus. I was "hiding among the baggage."

We have all been like Peter and Saul. Jesus told us in Mark 16:15 to go preach the good news to everyone everywhere! Let's go instead of hiding among the baggage! Hebrews 12:1 admonishes us, "Wherefore seeing we also are compassed about with so great a cloud of witnesses, let us lay aside every weight [the baggage], and the sin which doth so easily beset us, and let us run ["go ye"] with patience the race that is set before us."

The greatest, most important event that has ever taken place in your life was receiving Jesus into your heart. You became a new person, never to be the same again! The second greatest, most important event that will happen in your life is leading someone in a prayer that will change their eternal existence. The third greatest event in your life is teaching someone how to lead people to Jesus. Let's embrace the word, "Go preach," and produce a harvest beyond our wildest dreams!

You can get started today! You do not have to wait a single minute to start changing the world for Jesus Christ! I tried sharing my faith for many years without results. I would watch Christian television, see big-time soul winners being interviewed, and wish that one day I would be able to lead someone in a prayer to receive Jesus. I began asking God to help me become more effective in sharing my faith. What the Lord has taught me has been an ongoing process, and I know there is still more the Lord will show me. But I can share with you today how you can start sharing your faith.

And then [Jesus] told them, "Go into
all the world
and preach the Good News to
everyone [everywhere]."

Mark 16:15, *NLT*

CHAPTER 4

See Yourself
as God
Sees You!

Before you learn how to witness to others with the love of God, you must understand the importance of what you are saying. What have you been saying about yourself? What have you been saying concerning your ability to witness to others? In order to be an effective witness for Jesus, you must watch what you say about yourself.

Let me explain how your words affect your life.

> And Jesus said unto them, Because of your unbelief: for verily I say unto you, If ye have faith as a grain of mustard seed, ye shall say unto this mountain, Remove hence to yonder place; and it shall remove; and *nothing shall be impossible unto you* (Matthew 17:20).

Say this aloud: "With God all things are possible!"

> But Jesus beheld them, and said unto them, With men this is impossible; but *with God all things are possible* (Matthew 19:26).

Say it again: "With God all things are possible!"

> Jesus said unto him, If thou canst believe, *all things are possible* to him that believeth (Mark 9:23).

Say it again: "With God all things are possible!" Notice this scripture said that all things are possible to him that *believes*. Say this aloud: "I'm a believer! I can believe!"

> And Jesus looking upon them saith, With men it is impossible, but not with God: for *with God all things are possible* (Mark 10:27).

Say it again: "With God all things are possible!"

> For with God nothing shall be impossible (Luke 1:37).

Say it one more time: "With God all things are possible!"

After saying these scriptures, I'm sure you can feel faith stirring in your spirit. Romans 10:17 *(NKJV)* says, "Faith comes by hearing and hearing by the word of God." Speaking the Word of God aloud is called positive affirmation or confession. You should daily confess the Word. Positive statements found in the Word of God should be used to change the way you think about yourself and your situation.

Your mind responds to whatever words you give it. As a result, you eventually help to create the reality that matches your most predominant beliefs, attitudes and thoughts. By repeating positive confessions according to the Word of God every time a negative, self-defeating thought comes to mind, you can retrain your mind.

Romans 12:2 *(NLT)* says, "...let God transform you into a new person by changing the way you think." Then you will feel more confident and be a bold witness for Jesus Christ! Over time, old, limited thoughts and mental patterns that contributed to fear, doubt or timidity will lose their power and eventually stop arising altogether.

The Bible says in Proverbs 6:2, "Thou art snared with the words of thy mouth, thou art taken with the words of thy mouth." Your words have power over your life. Jesus put it this way in Matthew 12:37, "For by thy words thou shalt be justified, and by thy words thou shalt be condemned."

The Body of Christ has had a negative confession over the subject of evangelism. We must remember that our words rule us! Jesus said in Mark 11:23, "For verily I say unto you, That whosoever *shall say* unto this mountain, Be thou removed, and be thou cast into the sea; and *shall not doubt* in his heart, but *shall believe* that those things which *he saith* shall come to pass; he *shall have* whatsoever *he saith*."

Our problem is that we have been getting exactly what we have been saying. I have heard the following statements from the Body of Christ: "I can't witness." "I don't know how." "I'm afraid." "I don't feel led to share my faith." "I'm afraid of what my friends might think." "What will my family think?"

Your thoughts, whether negative or positive, create an inner image, or picture, on the inside of you. You begin to see failure or success in your life. Your words create a picture of victory or defeat. Your words become what you believe. You believe what you say because you know yourself better than any other person on the face of this earth.

When you look in the mirror, you have to see yourself the way God sees you. You have to find yourself in the Word of God. You do this by renewing your mind daily. In Romans 12:2 we are told not to conform to this world but be transformed by the renewing of our mind.

At this point, you might be thinking, *Riley, what does this have to do with sharing my faith?* This has everything to do with sharing Jesus! When we see ourselves as God sees us, we will do what He says we can do. Paul told us in Ephesians 4:22-24, "That ye put off concerning the *former conversation* the old man, which is corrupt according to the deceitful lusts; and *be renewed* in the spirit of your mind; and that ye put on the *new man,* which after God is created in righteousness and true holiness."

Let's stop talking like the world talks and renew our thinking to the Word of God. Let's put on the new man that will speak in line with righteousness and holy conversation! I want to share with you some scriptures you can confess over your life that will enable you to be a bold witness for Jesus Christ.

> **I can do all things through Christ which strengtheneth me (Philippians 4:13).**

Say this aloud: "I can do all things through Christ with His Anointing and His ability empowering me! I have the mind of Christ!"

> **For God did not give us a spirit of timidity (of cowardice, of craven and cringing and fawning fear), but (He has given us a spirit) of power and of love and of calm and well-balanced mind and discipline and self-control (2 Timothy 1:7, *AMP*).**

Say this aloud: "God did not give me a spirit of fear, but of power, love and a sound mind! I am not afraid to share my faith in Jesus' Name! Fear, I take authority over you in the Name of Jesus! You have no place in my life! I recognize you and render you helpless in the Name of Jesus! God did not make me timid or a coward!"

> **The wicked flee when no man pursueth: but the righteous are bold as a lion (Proverbs 28:1).**

Say this aloud: "I am as bold as a lion! The lost won't flee from me when I'm sharing the gospel! I pursue the lost at any cost!"

Let's read the account in Mark 9:17-27 *(MSG):*

> A man out of the crowd answered, "Teacher, I brought
> my mute son, made speechless by a demon, to you.
> Whenever it seizes him, it throws him to the ground.
> He foams at the mouth, grinds his teeth, and goes stiff
> as a board. I told your disciples, hoping they could
> deliver him, but they couldn't." Jesus said, "What a
> generation! No sense of God! How many times do I
> have to go over these things? How much longer do
> I have to put up with this? Bring the boy here." They
> brought him. When the demon saw Jesus, it threw
> the boy into a seizure, causing him to writhe on the
> ground and foam at the mouth. He asked the boy's
> father, "How long has this been going on?" "Ever
> since he was a little boy. Many times it pitches him
> into fire or the river to do away with him. If you can do
> anything, do it. Have a heart and help us!" Jesus said,
> "If? There are no 'ifs' among believers. Anything can
> happen." No sooner were the words out of his mouth
> than the father cried, "Then I believe. Help me with
> my doubts!" Seeing that the crowd was forming fast,
> Jesus gave the vile spirit its marching orders: "Dumb
> and deaf spirit, I command you—Out of him, and stay
> out!" Screaming, and with much thrashing about, it
> left. The boy was pale as a corpse, so people started
> saying, "He's dead." But Jesus, taking his hand, raised
> him. The boy stood up.

This is a great passage in the Bible of a man, like us, who heard the Word and faith began to rise in his heart. But when the man looked at the natural circumstances—his son foaming at the mouth and grinding his teeth—he began to doubt. We have all done this. We have all looked at the natural circumstances concerning witnessing.

Jesus told the man, "If there are no ifs, anything could happen!"

I want to ask you, "How long have you been saying, 'I can't witness,' 'I don't know how,' 'I'm afraid'?" I want to tell you today that if there are no ifs, anything can happen! If you have faith in your heart to share Jesus and do not doubt in your head, anything is possible!

 Say this aloud: "I can be an effective witness for Jesus!"

*We're not keeping this quiet,
not on your life.
Just like the psalmist who wrote,
"I believed it, so I said it,"
we say what we believe.*

2 Corinthians 4:13, *MSG*

CHAPTER 5

The Power
of Confession for
Soul Winners

Confessions are statements spoken out loud based on the Word of God that describe a desired result and which are repeated many times in order to imprint the spirit man with an image and trigger it into action. Let's take a look at a few scriptures about the spirit man.

> The spirit of man is the lamp of the Lord, searching all the inner depths of his heart (Proverbs 20:27, *NKJV*).

> The spirit of a man will sustain him in sickness (Proverbs 18:14, *NKJV*).

> For out of the abundance of the heart the mouth speaks (Matthew 12:34, *NKJV*).

Many times I have heard people make negative statements about soul winning. Unfortunately, this brings doubt and fear in regards to winning the lost. We have to renew our mind to what the Bible says. Statements we say can either build or destroy our lives; they can bring positive or negative results. Let's take a look at two scriptures concerning the words or statements we say.

The words you say will either acquit you or condemn you (Matthew 12:37, *NLT*).

By faith we understand that the entire universe was formed at God's command, that what we now see did not come from anything that can be seen (Hebrews 11:3, *NLT*).

God created this entire universe with His words! And He expects us to use His words spoken out of our mouths to put us over in life. I want you to imagine yourself going out to win souls with your church. They have been seeing people get saved, something you have never done before. You can start using the *Pocket Reference for Soul Winning* card (download this from my website at www.rileystephenson.com). At the same time, you are confessing, "I can do this! I can do all things through Christ. I can do it!" You keep thinking and believing that you are going to see people saved. What are you actually doing? You are repeating positive confessions.

Speaking the Word of God will influence you, other people, events and circumstances. It might seem strange to you, but speaking the Word of God will also influence the people you meet, your circumstances, and the events you encounter. Sometimes the confessions work fast, but more often they need time. Repeating positive confessions a few minutes a day and then thinking negatively the rest of the time neutralizes the effects of the positive words. You have to refuse negative thoughts; otherwise you will not attain positive results.

Many times we mentally repeat negative statements without even being aware of the process. We use them when we tell ourselves that we cannot do something, that we are too lazy, or when we believe we are going to fail. The mind always accepts and follows what we tell it, whether it is good or bad for us. So, why not choose only positive statements?

In the beginning, I would advise you to repeat scriptures that are not too long so they will be easier to remember. Find a place where you can get quiet and concentrate. It is important to confess in the present tense, not the future tense. If you say, "I will be a soul winner," you are actually telling yourself that some day you will be a soul winner. It is better and more effective to say, "I am a soul winner now." The spirit man will work overtime to make this happen now, in the present. The dominating thoughts of your mind will eventually reproduce themselves in outward, physical action and will gradually transform themselves into physical reality. Before you know it, you will be winning people to Jesus every day!

I win people to Jesus every day!

Soul Winners' Confessions

Say the following out loud:

- People are pouring into my life!

- Greater is He that is in me, than he that is in the world! (1 John 4:4)

- I am getting people saved every day!

- The spirit of fear has no power over me! (2 Timothy 1:7)

- I preach the good news!

- I am a people magnet!

- I have favor with people! (Psalm 5:12)

- If God is for me, no man can be against me! (Romans 8:31)

- The love of God flows through me! (Romans 5:5)

- I see people as God sees them!

- I am a minister of reconciliation! (2 Corinthians 5:18)

- I am wise because I win souls! (Proverbs 11:30)

- I share Jesus with everyone everywhere! (Mark 16:15)

- I am the righteousness of God in Christ! (2 Corinthians 5:21)

- I am a child of God, and a joint heir with Jesus! (Romans 8:17, Galatians 3:26)

- I am more than a conqueror! (Romans 8:37)

- I am a royal priesthood! (1 Peter 2:9)

- I am triumphant in Jesus' Name! (2 Corinthians 2:14)

- I am delivered from the power of darkness! (Colossians 1:13)

Whatever is in God is in you and me.
Keep reminding yourself of that.
It is the process of the renewing of
the mind that will bring you
to a place of total deliverance and
freedom from fear.

—George Pearsons

For though we walk in the flesh,
we do not war after the flesh:
(For the weapons of our warfare
are not carnal, but mighty through
God to the pulling down of
strong holds.)

2 Corinthians 10:3-4

CHAPTER 6

You Are Empowered to Preach the Gospel!

O n the day you were born again, you became anointed, empowered, authorized and chosen! You are empowered and authorized by Jesus Christ, the Savior of the world, to preach the good news! Everything you need to fulfill God's will for your life is on the inside of you right now.

This very day God has been speaking to you about your dreams and desires. Don't give up! You can do it! When you realize who you are and what you can do in line with God's Word, you are on the first step of your destiny. Your destiny was planned by God before you were ever born.

O Lord, you have examined my heart and know everything about me. You know when I sit down or stand up. You know my thoughts even when I'm far away. You see me when I travel and when I rest at home. You know everything I do. You know what I am going to say even before I say it, Lord. You go before me and follow me. You place your hand of blessing on my head. Such knowledge is too wonderful for me, too great for me to understand! I can never escape from your Spirit! I can never get away from your presence! If I go up to heaven, you are there; if I go down to the

> grave, you are there. If I ride the wings of the morning, if I dwell by the farthest oceans, even there your hand will guide me, and your strength will support me. I could ask the darkness to hide me and the light around me to become night—but even in darkness I cannot hide from you. To you the night shines as bright as day. Darkness and light are the same to you. You made all the delicate, inner parts of my body and knit me together in my mother's womb. Thank you for making me so wonderfully complex! Your workmanship is marvelous—how well I know it. You watched me as I was being formed in utter seclusion, as I was woven together in the dark of the womb. You saw me before I was born. Every day of my life was recorded in your book. Every moment was laid out before a single day had passed (Psalm 139:1-16, *NLT*).

You are on the right path today! God knows you! He knows everything about you. That's why He would never tell you to do something you weren't empowered, authorized and chosen to do!

Let's look at Psalm 138:8: "The Lord will work out his plans for my life" *(NLT)*. We are God's masterpiece. He has created us new in Christ Jesus so that we can do the good things He planned for us long ago. He made us brand new in Christ! We have learned from Brother Kenneth Copeland that *Christ* means "the Anointed One" and the *anointing* is "the burden-removing, yoke-destroying power of God."

So we can say aloud: "God created me new in the Anointed One, and through His Anointing—that burden-removing, yoke-destroying power of God—I can do the good things He has planned for me. God has made every provision I need to do what He has *empowered and authorized* me to do! I can do it!"

Mark 16:15 is known as the Great Commission. In the *New Living Translation*, Jesus says, "Go into all the world and preach the Good

News to everyone." We are instructed by Jesus to witness to everyone, everywhere.

God says, "Go preach!"

You say, "Where?"

God says, "Everywhere!"

You say, "Who do I preach to?"

God says, "Everyone!"

But when we are standing face-to-face with our neighbor, mailman, pizza guy, convenience-store clerk, or fast-food clerk, we look at the natural circumstances and think, *What if they reject me?*

When we begin to doubt, we are saying, "Hello, Mr. Doubt, come right on in here and hand me that bag of lies." We just opened up the door to Mr. Doubt and Mrs. Unbelief. This Mr. and Mrs. team has robbed the Church for years. God says, "Go." The devil says to you, "They might reject you and think you're crazy." God says, "Go." The devil says to you, "You haven't memorized enough scriptures." God says, "Go." The devil says to you, "He looks like a Christian." Jesus told us to go to *everyone, everywhere!*

The Church has been lied to. Now let me ask you, "Who is the father of lies?" John 8:44 says, "...for he [the devil] is a liar, and the father of it." We just learned from Mark 9 that if there are no ifs, anything can happen. Verse 23 says, "...If thou canst believe, all things are possible to him that believeth." We cannot let Satan keep us from sharing our faith!

You can be an effective witness for Jesus! You can shake your city with the gospel! You can shake your nation for Jesus! You can change the world! God is looking for men and women to take their place in the Body of Christ. I believe you are the very one God will use for this end-time harvest of souls.

We are bold so they may live.

—Riley Stephenson

Say not ye, There are yet four months, and then cometh harvest? behold, I say unto you, Lift up your eyes, and look on the fields; for they are white already to harvest. And he that reapeth receiveth wages, and gathereth fruit unto life eternal: that both he that soweth and he that reapeth may rejoice together. And herein is that saying true, One soweth, and another reapeth. I sent you to reap that whereon ye bestowed no labour: other men laboured, and ye are entered into their labours.

John 4:35-38

Motivated by Love

I once asked God, "How do You save the world?" He took me to John 3:16-17:

> For God so loved the world, that he gave his only begotten Son, that whosoever believeth in him should not perish, but have everlasting life. For God sent not his Son into the world to condemn the world; but that the world through him might be saved.

God loved this lost and hell-bound world so much that He gave His Son! All He requires is for us to believe. What does it mean *to believe?* It means "to take or to grasp." Believe that you can go to this lost world and take the message that God loves them. You can change your world for Jesus!

John 3:17 says that Jesus did not come to condemn the world. So if Jesus did not condemn, we should not condemn. The people who are not saved know they need a Savior. They have tried to find peace in many different ways. Instead of condemning the people, we love them. You may be thinking, *How do we love the people?* Let's look at what the Bible says:

> Love is patient and kind. Love is not jealous or boastful or proud or rude. It does not demand its own way. It is not irritable, and it keeps no record of being wronged. It does not rejoice about injustice but rejoices whenever the truth wins out. Love never gives up, never loses faith, is always hopeful, and endures through every circumstance (1 Corinthians 13:4-7, *NLT*).

Love will last forever. God is love, and God is in you! So you are love. When we witness, we are patient and kind. When we witness, we are not proud or rude. When we witness, we do not demand our own way (especially when we are talking to people from other denominations or religions). We are not irritable. And when people mock or yell at us, we keep no record of that. We rejoice when the truth wins! We never give up on people! We never lose faith in people! Our love will last forever!

The Bible says in 1 John 4:18 there is no fear in love, and perfect love casts out fear. One of the No. 1 reasons why people don't witness is fear. So according to the Word, if there is a fear problem, there is a love problem. Perfect love will cast out all fear.

If you love me and it's obvious I need Jesus, you will minister to me regardless of how scary I am or how smelly I am. Let's say the person God wants you to witness to isn't wearing a suit or looking pretty at your church. Let's be real and stop making excuses! God has poured out His love into our hearts by the Holy Spirit. We just need to improve in our love walk toward others and start seeing people as God sees them. Perfect love will cast out fear! Love looks past imperfections and sees what is perfect. Love sees the need and has the solution. Love goes to a lost world regardless of the weather.

One night I was taking a team out on an evangelistic event. I received a phone call from someone before we left. The person said,

"Riley, I'm not going out tonight because it's storming." After the phone call ended, the Lord spoke up and said, *It's storming in someone's life tonight, and you have the answer to the problem.* Love sees that co-worker who uses profanity and goes to him and befriends him, instead of saying, "Don't use profanity in my presence."

Someone once said, "People don't care how much you know until they know how much you care." When I share Jesus with people, my motivation is love. Love gives and never gives up! I thank God He never gave up on me! God is in the people business. God is not trying to keep people out of His house, but instead He is trying to get them in by the thousands!

*And above all things have fervent
love for one another,
for "love will cover a multitude
of sins."*

1 Peter 4:8, *NKJV*

For you have been called to live in freedom, my brothers and sisters. But don't use your freedom to satisfy your sinful nature. Instead, use your freedom to serve one another in love. For the whole law can be summed up in this one command: "Love your neighbor as yourself."

Galatians 5:13-14, *NLT*

CHAPTER 8

The Approach

There are many ways to share Jesus; the best way is the one you will use. I want to share with you the approach I use. This approach produces successful results every time! You have to realize it is not you who causes the salvation. It is not you who has to make something happen. Jesus told us to go and tell the good news!

Initially, when you see someone, smile. Can you smile? Get up, look in the mirror, and smile. I've heard it said that a smile improves your face value. So, when you see someone, smile.

The next thing I do is ask them if they live in the area. If they say yes, then I ask them if they go to church in the area. Then I ask them the following: "If you died today, where would you go?" If they say, "Heaven," I ask them, "Why would God let you in?" If they say, "I don't know," or have another answer than Jesus is their Lord and Savior, I share with them the following scriptures from the *Pocket Reference for Soul Winning* card (download at www.rileystephenson.com):

All have sinned (Romans 3:23, *NIV*).

The wages of sin is death, but the gift of God is eternal life (Romans 6:23, *NIV*).

Whosoever shall call upon the name of the Lord shall be saved (Romans 10:13).

After I have shared these scriptures with them, I extend my hand and tell them to pray this prayer aloud with me: "Heavenly Father, I believe Jesus died on the cross for me and rose again. I give You my life. I want Jesus Christ to come into my life and into my heart. Amen." If they were already saved, I tell them that Paul told Timothy to "do the work of an evangelist" (see 2 Timothy 4:5). They can do the same; they can tell others about Jesus!

Ask Questions:

Do you live in the area?

Do you go to church in the area?

If you died right now, where would you go?

If God were to say, "Why would I let you in?" what would you tell Him?

The Bible Reads:

Romans 3:23: All have sinned.

Romans 6:23: The wages of sin is death, but the gift of God is eternal life.

Romans 10:13: Whosoever shall call upon the Name of the Lord shall be saved.

The Prayer:

"Heavenly Father, I believe Jesus died on the cross for me and rose again. I give You my life. I want Jesus Christ to come into my life and into my heart. Amen."

You can also use a tract to share the good news with people. I wrote a tract called, *You Are Loved!* It has also produced successful results in witnessing to people. I would like to share this tract with you.

You Are Loved!

God loves you! Love never gives up! God's love for you endures through every circumstance—no matter what you have done in the past. The Bible says in 2 Corinthians 5:19 that God is no longer counting people's sins against them. When God sent Jesus to die on the cross, He paid the price for our sin.

You are forgiven! The only sin that will keep you out of heaven is not believing in Jesus. All you have to do to know you will go to heaven when you die is: Confess with your mouth that Jesus is Lord and believe in your heart that God raised Him from the dead, and you will be saved (Romans 10:9, *NIV).*

Pray this prayer: Heavenly Father, I believe that Jesus is Your Son. You sent Him to pay the price for my sin. I believe You raised Him from the dead and He is Lord. Today, I make Him my Lord. Jesus, come into my life!

As you can see, I use different ways to share my faith. The best way is the one *you* will use! After they pray the prayer of salvation with me, I invite them to my church if they live in my area. I explain to them that the decision they just made was the best decision they will ever make. I ask them who has been praying for them. Sometimes they tell me a mother or a grandmother has been praying for them. So I tell them to give that person a call.

Once they are saved, I tell them to read their Bible. Everything they need to know about God is in the Bible. Then they need to attend a church; they need to find a place where they are loved and accepted. Finally, they need to follow God's commandment of love, to love their neighbor as themselves.

*Lukewarm is not a luxury given to
those who endeavor and commit to
carrying the title of a Christian.*

—Vanessa Dawn Adams

And he saith unto them, Follow me, and I will make you fishers of men.

Matthew 4:19

For though I be free from all men, yet have I made myself servant unto all, that I might gain the more.

1 Corinthians 9:19

CHAPTER 9

Tips Before You Go

The following tips will help you have a successful witnessing experience every time!

Set a Goal and Step Out in Faith

We have the assurance that every time we share our faith someone will get saved. The Bible says in Isaiah 55:11 that God's Word will not return void. Setting a goal will help you to stay motivated. Setting a "number of souls goal" before you go out will help you to plan and avoid distractions that will try to get you off course.

Jesus said in John 4 the people are ready! Learn from every experience. This will make you a stronger and better witness!

Overcome Fear-Filled Thoughts

Second Timothy 1:7 in *The Amplified Bible* says, "For God did not give us a spirit of timidity (of cowardice, of craven and cringing and fawning fear), but [He has given us a spirit] of power and of love and of calm and well-balanced mind and discipline and self-control." You can overcome fear-filled thoughts! One of the biggest fears in witnessing is the fear of failure. You cannot fail. God, Jesus and the Holy Spirit are on the inside of you, helping you tell the good news! It's not up to you; it's up to God, Jesus and the Holy Spirit to get the person saved. You can start out by passing out tracts. Doing this will build your confidence and help you succeed in soul winning.

Talk to Everyone

God wants you to talk to everyone! He would never say, "Don't talk to that person." When you are out witnessing, listen to what is going on inside of you. You made a decision to witness and the Lord says, "Go!" He will show you a person, and you are on your way. However, as you "go," you may hear, *Don't talk to that person. He looks like a Christian.* Or you may hear, *That guy could beat you up!* Are those thoughts from the Lord? No, I don't think so. Jesus said, "Go preach to everyone everywhere!"

Dealing With Rejection

When they reject you, they reject Jesus. When you witness and they yell at you or snub you, they are not rejecting you, they are rejecting Jesus. You have planted the seed of the Word of God into their heart. Don't take it personally! They rejected you not because of what you did—it was a result of what was going on inside of them. All God asks us to do is to be obedient! It's His job to save them! It's our job to go!

Don't *Ask* the People to Pray

After you have shared the Word of God, reach out your hand and say, "Pray with me." Don't ask the person. If the person doesn't want to, he will say, "No." I never ask the person I am talking to if he is ready to pray. The lost person sees things merely from a human point of view. The Bible says in 1 Corinthians 2:14 that the natural man thinks the things of God are foolish. Spiritual things must be spiritually discerned. When I share the Word, I am speaking directly to a person's spirit. Then

I reach out my hand and say, "Pray this prayer with me." The person will tell me if he doesn't want to.

Compel Them!

The word *compel* simply means "to urge." Ask, ask and ask the questions! Jesus said in Luke 14:23, "And the lord said unto the servant, Go out into the highways and hedges, and compel them to come in, that my house may be filled." If someone says, "I'm in a hurry," you can say, "I'll walk with you." You can press but remember that love is not rude!

The Word Speaks to a Person's Spirit

The Word is what speaks to a person's spirit man. The Bible says in Isaiah 55:11 that God's Word will not return void. Also, in Jeremiah 1:12 we learn that God watches over His Word to perform it. If all a person hears is, "Jesus," we have a promise from the Word of God that one day that person will be saved. First Peter 1:23 calls the Word of God "incorruptible seed." This seed will produce a mighty harvest!

Dealing With Other Evangelistic Approaches

There are many people sharing the gospel. And there are many different ways to share your faith. I have found the best approach is the one you will use on a daily basis. If someone does not agree with your approach, walk in love! Do not argue with people who use other approaches. The Bible says that every joint supplies and causes growth for the benefit of the body (see Ephesians 4:16).

Don't Debate With People

One time I was talking to a man from another religion. I was using the scriptures and asking him the questions; I thought I was doing all the right things. But I was getting nowhere with this man. All the while, people were walking all around us. The Lord gave me a good example of what was happening. He reminded me of when a lure gets caught on something while fishing. You keep pulling and pulling while moving the rod one way and then the other. He said the best thing to do is cut the line and tie another lure on. He said, *You planted the seed and it will harvest! There were people all around you who were lost, just like there are fish all around a lure that is hung up!*

The Survey Approach

You can use the questions like a survey. You could even use me as an excuse to do it. Just say, "Hey, this guy wrote a book and told me to ask you these questions. Do you mind if I ask you a few questions?" Make a list of the questions, put them on a clipboard or whatever you need to do in order to feel comfortable, and then "Go!"

Etiquette in Talking to Employees on the Job

Don't talk to employees if they are busy with customers. Talking to someone who is busy with customers is not being a good witness and will often cause a scene. When people are working, they are getting paid by their employer to do the job they were hired to do. When you are in line and people are waiting on you, that is not a good time to share your faith. If no one is around, then that is a different story. God will show you!

Believe for Favor With People

The Bible says in Psalm 5:12 that God's favor surrounds us. Jesus had so much favor everywhere He went. He increased in wisdom and stature, and in favor with God and man (see Luke 2:52). Pray every day for the favor of God to go before you! Favor will bring people across your path who need Jesus, and you will have just the right words to say to them!

Dealing With Civil Authorities

When you are sharing your faith in a mall or at a grocery store, someone could get offended. This has happened to me. They might tell a security guard or a police officer. *The Message* Bible says, "Don't be upset when they haul you before the civil authorities" (see Matthew 10:18). If you are in a mall or somewhere else where there is security or police, you should obey what they tell you. Remember, you are a witness wherever you are!

Smile and Be Friendly

The best thing you can do when handing out a tract or sharing your faith is to smile and be friendly. Act excited when people are talking to you. Stay focused on what they are saying. Don't look around. Be a good listener! Their eternal destiny could be at stake! Finally, have a good time! Every area of my life has changed so much since I started sharing my faith. God wants to do the same in your life. I challenge you to take these principles, apply them, and see thousands come to know Jesus as their Lord! You can do it! Remember that *all things* are possible to those who believe!

*And the lord said unto the servant,
Go out into the highways and
hedges, and compel them to come
in, that my house may be filled.*

Luke 14:23

CHAPTER 10

Witnessing at
Fast-Food
Restaurants

Most fast-food restaurants have approximately two minutes from the time you pull up until the time you leave to get your order out to you. When I go through a drive-through, I look for the person's name tag. I call the person by name to make it personal.

I say "Hey Joe, do you live in this area? Do you go to church anywhere? If you died today, do you know where you would go?" If Joe says, "I don't know," or "I hope I'd go to heaven," I stick out my hand and tell Joe to pray this prayer after me: "Jesus, come into my heart. I believe You died on the Cross and God raised You from the dead. Change my life and make me new in Jesus' Name. Amen." This can be done in less than 60 seconds!

Soon after Sept. 11, 2001, I was at a drive-in restaurant where the servers come out to your car. A waitress named Brandi brought my food. She took my money, and I gave her a generous tip. She began to talk about the tragedy that had just happened in New York. She seemed afraid of what was going on. I let her talk until she was finished.

Then I said to her, "Brandi, if you were to die today, where would you go?" She said, "Hell!" I said, "Why hell?" She said, "I'm not living the way I should." I said, "Brandi, you can go to heaven. God loves you and He has a wonderful plan for your life. Pray this prayer with me." At that moment, she grabbed my hand and accepted Jesus as her Lord and Savior. When we finished praying, I asked her, "Where is Jesus?" She said, "In my heart." Glory to God! Jude 23 in *The Amplified Bible* says, "Strive to save others, snatching them out of the fire." That day Brandi was snatched out of the fire!

One day I drove up to the speaker at a fast-food restaurant and a man walked up to me before I could order. He asked me if I wanted to buy some designer cologne. He gave me a long sales pitch. I said, "Hey, you asked me a couple of questions; now let me ask you one. If you died today, where would you go?" He said, "I don't know but I know it's not good." I stuck out my hand and he prayed and asked Jesus to come into his heart! I ordered my food, drove up to the first window, and paid for my food. Then I asked the girl at the window, "If you died today, where would you go?" She said, "Hell." I asked her why and she said that she was a bad girl. I told her she could go to heaven. I reached out my hand. She grabbed it and prayed to ask Jesus into her heart.

I drove up to the second window to get my food. The girl there got saved. I drove back around to give the first girl a Bible and saw the man with the cologne talking to two of his friends. I told him to ask his friends the question I asked him. They didn't know where they would go! I grabbed their hands and led them in a prayer of salvation!

One Friday, I made signs that said we were giving away free food on Saturday. I took the signs to an apartment complex. As I was putting one of these signs on a bulletin board there, a young man came up to me and asked for a ride. I said, "Sure." He needed a ride to find a job. I took him to several fast-food places. I asked if he was hungry, and he said yes. So we went to a local Mexican restaurant.

As we talked there at the restaurant, I asked him if he knew where he would go if he died that day. He said he believed he would go to hell. Then he shared with me, "The only thing preventing me from committing suicide is that I know I would go to hell." I shared some scriptures with him and encouraged him. Then I looked at him and said, "Today, everything changes!" I took him back to his apartment and he prayed and asked Jesus into his heart.

You can do this! Greater is He that is in you than he that is in the world! Who told you that you could not be an effective witness for Jesus? Some of the excuses I hear all the time are, "I am afraid to witness," or "I'm afraid I don't know enough scriptures," or "I'm afraid I will lose my friends." Let's look at the first time man became afraid.

The serpent was the shrewdest of all the wild animals the Lord God had made. One day he asked the woman, "Did God really say you must not eat the fruit from any of the trees in the garden?" "Of course we may eat fruit from the trees in the garden," the woman replied. "It's only the fruit from the tree in the middle of the garden that we are not allowed to eat. God said, 'You must not eat it or even touch it; if you do, you will die.'" "You won't die!" the serpent replied to the woman. "God knows that your eyes will be opened as soon as you eat it, and you will be like God, knowing both good and evil." The woman was convinced. She saw that the tree was beautiful and its fruit looked delicious, and she wanted the wisdom it would give her. So she took some of the fruit and ate it. Then she gave some to her husband, who was with her, and he ate it, too. At that moment their eyes were opened, and they suddenly felt shame at their nakedness. So they sewed fig leaves together to cover themselves. When the cool evening breezes were blowing, the man and his wife heard the Lord God walking about in the garden. So they hid from the Lord God among the trees. Then the Lord God called to the man, "Where are you?" He replied, "I heard you walking in the garden, so I hid. I was afraid because I was naked." "Who told you that you were naked?" the Lord God asked... (Genesis 3:1-11, *NLT).*

As you are reading this book, your faith is being built up. I know some of you have already started talking to the people around you. You are getting excited about going out into the world!

I want you to understand the moment you decide to talk to someone, Satan will say to you, "You can't witness to that person. That person will chew you up and spit you out." He will say, "That person is part of a world religion. You haven't read the book on that yet." It happens all the time. Or you will hear, "Those people look saved." Another one is, "You can't witness to them; they are a different race. They won't understand you."

Are these thoughts coming from the throne room of heaven? No, they most certainly are not! Jesus is saying the same thing today as He said more than 2,000 years ago. He is telling us to go into all the world and tell the good news!

*Knowing therefore
the terror of the Lord,
we persuade men.*

2 Corinthians 5:11

CHAPTER 11

Praying
for the
Harvest

L et's take a look at a few scriptures on prayer.

Pray at all times (on every occasion, in every season) in the Spirit, with all [manner of] prayer and entreaty. To that end keep alert and watch with strong perseverance, interceding in behalf of all the saints (God's consecrated people) (Ephesians 6:18, *AMP*).

So too the [Holy] Spirit comes to our aid and bears us up in our weakness; for we do not know what prayer to offer nor how to offer it worthily as we ought, but the Spirit Himself goes to meet our supplication and pleads in our behalf with unspeakable yearnings and groanings too deep for utterance (Romans 8:26, *AMP*).

Put me in remembrance [Put God in remembrance of His Word] (Isaiah 43:26).

Those scriptures reveal to us there are many different ways that we can pray, but they are all to be in the spirit. Many people think that praying in the spirit means praying in tongues. However, praying in the spirit is not limited to praying in tongues.

James 5:16 in *The Amplified Bible* says, "The earnest (heartfelt, continued) prayer of a righteous man makes tremendous power available [dynamic in its working]." The prayer that brings power is the prayer that comes from your heart, which is your spirit. The Bible does not say the "*head*felt" prayer of a righteous man makes tremendous power available.

The instruction given to us in Proverbs 3:5-6 is important to remember and heed when praying: "Trust in the Lord with all thine heart; and lean not unto thine own understanding. In all thy ways acknowledge him, and he shall direct thy paths."

Let the Holy Spirit lead you in what to focus on. Pray the Word and pray in tongues, following the unction of God. First John 2:20, 27 says you have been given an unction of the Holy One that will live in you forever. That unction will lead you and teach you.

How do you follow the unction? Follow the presence and Anointing of God. Do you sense His presence more when praying in tongues or praying the Word? Do you sense His presence when praying for one area versus another? Depend on the Holy Spirit who is your Helper and your Guide. He is the great Intercessor.

Your primary goal in prayer is to become aware of God's presence. In prayer, always consciously be aware that you are talking to your Father God. Hebrews 11:6 says, "But without faith it is impossible to please him: for he that cometh to God must believe that he is, and that he is a rewarder of them that diligently seek him."

You can use the following as a tool to assist you in praying for the harvest, but please do not do so without engaging your heart. I believe God will use it to spark things in your heart. You do not have to cover the entire chapter in one hour or session of prayer. This chapter will be especially useful in helping your group pray in unity.

How to Pray for the Harvest

Genesis 1 and Hebrews 2 reveal to us that God has given mankind power and authority in the earth. He has limited Himself to our prayers. John Wesley said it best: "It seems that God cannot do anything on earth unless someone asks Him."

Pray for the Lost

God has great plans for each person. He longs to intervene and act on behalf of His beloved creation, mankind. Ezekiel 22:30 says, "And I sought for a man among them, that should make up the hedge, and stand in the gap before me for the land, that I should not destroy it: but I found none."

God is still seeking for men who will stand in the gap for those who are lost and without God. Their sin of resisting God is separating them from Him, calling out for judgment. God longs to pour out His love and mercy on them and is searching for people who will intercede on their behalf and give Him a legal entrance into their lives.

Let's take a look at a few scriptures that will help us in praying for the lost.

> The Lord is...not willing that any should perish, but that all should come to repentance (2 Peter 3:9).

> And this is the confidence (the assurance, the privilege of boldness) which we have in Him: [we are sure] that if we ask anything (make any request) according to His will (in agreement with His own plan), He listens to and hears us. And if (since) we [positively] know that He listens to us in whatever we ask, we also know

> [with settled and absolute knowledge] that we have
> [granted us as our present possessions] the requests
> made of Him (1 John 5:14-15, *AMP).*
>
> And Jesus answering saith unto them, Have faith in
> God. For verily I say unto you, That whosoever shall
> say unto this mountain, Be thou removed, and be thou
> cast into the sea; and shall not doubt in his heart, but
> shall believe that those things which he saith shall
> come to pass; he shall have whatsoever he saith.
> Therefore I say unto you, What things soever ye desire,
> when ye pray, believe that ye receive them, and ye
> shall have them (Mark 11:22-24).

In Psalm 2:8 God says, "Ask of me, and I will give thee the [nations] for thine inheritance, and the uttermost parts of the earth for thy possession." If we can ask God for nations and He will give them to us, we can ask Him for neighborhoods and cities. The word translated in our Bibles as "nations" and sometimes translated as "heathen" simply means *ethnic people groups.*

God has a wonderful plan for each person. He longs for them to walk in that plan and experience His love and goodness. We are simply lifting His desire back up to Him, giving Him a legal right to intervene in their lives. Since it is His desire to meet each one where they are with His love, we know that when we pray we can expect God to answer and grant us our requests.

Pray for the Laborers to Be Thrust Into the Fields

Let's take a look at a few scriptures.

> After these things the Lord appointed other seventy
> also, and sent them two and two before his face into
> every city and place, whither he himself would come.

Therefore said he unto them, The harvest truly is great, but the labourers are few: pray ye therefore the Lord of the harvest, that he would send forth labourers into his harvest (Luke 10:1-2).

When He saw the throngs, He was moved with pity and sympathy for them, because they were bewildered (harassed and distressed and dejected and helpless), like sheep without a shepherd. Then He said to His disciples, The harvest is indeed plentiful, but the laborers are few. So pray to the Lord of the harvest to force out and thrust laborers into His harvest (Matthew 9:36-38, *AMP).*

It is one thing to be sent out by a person—but we believe that our teams are being sent out and thrust out by God. We believe that the same love and compassion that moved in Jesus is moving the members of the Body of Christ.

Pray for Utterance for the Laborers

And [pray] also for me, that [freedom of] utterance may be given me, that I may open my mouth to proclaim boldly the mystery of the good news (the Gospel), for which I am an ambassador...[Pray] that I may declare it boldly and courageously, as I ought to do (Ephesians 6:19-20, *AMP).*

I thank my God at all times for you because of the grace (the favor and spiritual blessing) of God which was bestowed on you in Christ Jesus, [so] that in Him in every respect you were enriched, in full power and readiness of speech [to speak of your faith] and complete knowledge and illumination [to give you full insight into its meaning] (1 Corinthians 1:4-5, *AMP).*

Whoever speaks, [let him do it as one who utters] oracles of God; whoever renders service (ministers), [let him do it] as with the strength which God furnishes abundantly, so that in all things God may be glorified through Jesus Christ... (1 Peter 4:11, *AMP*).

For I am well assured and indeed know that through your prayers and a bountiful supply of the Spirit of Jesus Christ (the Messiah) this will turn out for my preservation (for the spiritual health and welfare of my own soul) and avail toward the saving work of the Gospel. This is in keeping with my own eager desire and persistent expectation and hope, that I shall not disgrace myself nor be put to shame in anything; but that with the utmost freedom of speech and unfailing courage, now as always heretofore, Christ (the Messiah) (the Anointed One and His Anointing) will be magnified and get glory and praise in this body of mine and be boldly exalted in my person, whether through (by) life or through (by) death (Philippians 1:19-20, *AMP*).

...Yet in [the strength of] our God we summoned courage to proclaim to you unfalteringly the good news (the Gospel)... (1 Thessalonians 2:2, *AMP*).

Pray for the Presence and Power of God to Accompany the Words of the Laborers

And He said to them, Go into all the world and preach and publish openly the good news (the Gospel) to every creature [of the whole human race]. He who believes...and is baptized will be saved...but he who does not believe...will be condemned. And these attesting signs will accompany those who believe:

in My name they will drive out demons; they will speak in new languages; They will pick up serpents; and [even] if they drink anything deadly, it will not hurt them; they will lay their hands on the sick, and they will get well. So then the Lord Jesus, after He had spoken to them, was taken up into heaven and He sat down at the right hand of God. And they went out and preached everywhere, while the Lord kept working *with them* and confirming the message by the attesting signs and miracles that closely accompanied [it]. Amen (so be it) (Mark 16:15-20, *AMP).*

And the presence of the Lord was with them with power, so that a great number [learned] to believe (to adhere to and trust in and rely on the Lord) and turned and surrendered themselves to Him (Acts 11:21, *AMP).*

For what we preach is not ourselves but Jesus Christ as Lord, and ourselves [merely] as your servants (slaves) for Jesus' sake. For God Who said, Let light shine out of darkness, has shone in our hearts so as [to beam forth] the Light for the illumination of the knowledge of the majesty and glory of God [as it is manifest in the Person and is revealed] in the face of Jesus Christ (the Messiah). However, we possess this precious treasure [the divine Light of the Gospel] in [frail, human] vessels of earth, that the grandeur and exceeding greatness of the power may be shown to be from God and not from ourselves (2 Corinthians 4:5-7, *AMP).*

Pray for the Word to Grow and to Spread

> Furthermore, brethren, do pray for us, that the Word
> of the Lord may speed on (spread rapidly and run its
> course) and be glorified (extolled) and triumph, even as
> [it has done] with you. And that we may be delivered
> from perverse (improper, unrighteous) and wicked
> (actively malicious) men, for not everybody has faith
> and is held by it (2 Thessalonians 3:1-2, *AMP*).

> Thus the Word of the Lord...grew and spread and
> intensified, prevailing mightily (Acts 19:20, *AMP*).

But where sin abounded, grace did
much more abound:
That as sin hath reigned unto death,
even so might grace reign through
righteousness unto eternal life by
Jesus Christ our Lord.

Romans 5:20-21

CHAPTER 12

Salvation
Stories

The following are testimonies of many whose own lives have been changed as they've accepted the call to win the lost and make disciples. These are soul winners of all ages and walks of life (some of them children) who trained with me in equipping themselves to share their faith effectively and with great joy!

"On Friday night, I had a very memorable salvation experience. I spoke to a group of four teenagers (two boys and two girls). I asked them if they knew where they would go if they died that night. The two girls started jumping up and down saying, 'This is great! This is wonderful! We have been praying for this!' The two boys occasionally went to a church but didn't know where they would go when they died. I led both of them in a salvation prayer. The two girls explained that they had been praying for their boyfriends, that they would get saved. Praise the Lord! It was a divine appointment."

"On Saturday, I walked by customer service at the mall. Even though the mall was very busy, no one was waiting in line. One guy was behind the counter. I walked up to him and he said to me, 'Do you have a question?' What a setup! I said, 'As a matter of fact, I do have a question. Do you know where you'd go if you died tonight?' He looked at me kind of dumbfounded and said, 'In the ground.' I said, 'Did you know you can be sure you would go to heaven? In Romans it says that the wages of sin is death, but the gift of God is eternal life. And if you confess with your mouth the Lord Jesus and believe in your heart that God raised Him from the dead, you'll be saved and go to heaven.' Then I reached out my hand and said, 'Pray this prayer with me.' And he did. Then he said, 'Wow! That is amazing. Anytime you are here in this mall, would you please come by and talk to me about God?' I said that I would."

"At the mall, I walked up to a kiosk that was selling dog paraphernalia. I know it had to be God because I am not interested in animals, especially dogs! No one was at the kiosk except the two girls who were working there. I said that I was doing a survey in the mall on church attendance. I asked them if they attended church. One said, 'I grew up in a Christian home and used to go to church but now I work on Sundays.' The other girl said, 'I'm an agnostic, and I don't go to church.' I said, 'OK. That's good.' (I breezed right by her 'agnostic' comment.) Then I asked them where they would go if they died. The one girl who had grown up in a Christian home knew immediately she would go to heaven and said that Jesus lived in her heart. The other girl said, 'I don't know.' I reached out my hand and said, 'Pray this prayer now.' And she did! Well, she's not an agnostic now! God is so good! I look forward to seeing her in heaven one day."

"I went up to a man on a bench. He was reading a book. I asked if he wanted to know Jesus and he said yes. I prayed with him."

"I asked an elderly man if he lived in the area. He couldn't hear me so I spoke louder. I prayed with him to ask Jesus into his heart."

"Two women were standing together. I asked if they wanted Jesus and they said yes. So I prayed with them."

"On Friday night, I walked up to three teenage girls. I asked the questions and found out that two of the girls thought they were going to heaven because they did good things, and the other girl had no idea where she would go after she died. I went through the scriptures with them and started leading them in the prayer. About halfway through the prayer, the oldest girl's cell phone started ringing. She answered it and said, 'Excuse me, but I'm in the middle of saying a prayer, and I can't talk to you!' And she hung up! She then looked at me and asked me to finish the prayer. When we finished, they were so excited! They couldn't stop thanking me for talking to them! God is good!"

"On Friday night, I walked up to four teenagers. I shared with them the scriptures about what Jesus had done for them. And then I said, 'Repeat this prayer after me and you can know that you will go to heaven when you die.' One girl said, 'Do I have to pray out loud? Can't I just be quiet?' I said, 'Well, Jesus said that if you confess Him before men, He will confess you before the Father. So it is important to pray the prayer out loud.' She said, 'OK,' and then prayed with me."

"A group of us went to IHOP on Friday night. I walked up to a group of men at several tables. There were 11 men in all. They were in town just briefly doing some construction work. I asked them if they knew where they would go if they died that night. They were not sure. I shared the three scriptures from Romans and then all 11 men bowed their heads in IHOP and prayed and asked Jesus to come into their hearts.

"Praise God! God is good! We are bringing the good news of what Jesus has done to everyone everywhere! (Thanks, Riley, for always encouraging us to be bold for Jesus! I love it!)"

"I just had to share this story! A month ago, 9-year-old Jessica came to an Angel Food outreach. I saw in her a love for God and a desire to help people. I wanted to give her the opportunity to see what it was like to minister to people, so I invited her to another outreach. She came and had a good time. On the way home on the bus, she turned to me and said, 'I want Jesus to come into my heart.' I prayed with her.

"Well, just a few days ago, Jessica said to me, 'I want to go again to hand out boxes of food to people.' I said, 'OK, we are going this Saturday.' I didn't know it at the time, but a friend had invited her to the zoo that Saturday. She chose instead to hand out boxes of food to people.

"I gave her the *Pocket Reference for Soul Winning* card and went over it with her. She watched me pray with some people. Then she read from the card and ended up praying with about 10 people on Saturday. She kissed the card and said, 'I love this secret prayer. I want to pray it with everyone.'

"Today, I sat down with Jessica's mom to share with her what her daughter was doing. I showed her the card and told her that Jessica was leading people to Jesus. Her mom was so proud of her daughter! She was surprised at her daughter's boldness. Her mom was reminded of a time when she was a little girl, and someone took her to a place to minister to people. She never forgot that. She thought it was awesome that Jessica had the opportunity to go with me and minister the love of God to people!

"As we finished our conversation, Jessica walked up to us and saw the card lying on the table. She said to me, 'Did you pray the prayer with my mom?' I said, 'No, I was waiting for you to read the card to your mom.' Right in my office, Jessica read the card to her mom: 'Do you live in the area?' Her mom said, 'Yes.' 'Do you go to church in the area?' Her mom said, 'Sometimes.' 'If you died right now, where would you go?' Her mom said, 'To heaven.'

"Jessica went on, 'If God were to say, "Why should I let you in," what would you tell Him?' Her mom said, 'That I believe in God.' Jessica read the three scriptures from Romans and then said, 'Mom, repeat this prayer after me.' Jessica's mom prayed the prayer. Then Jessica said, 'Mom, now you are going to heaven with me! I am so glad!' It was such a beautiful thing to watch this 9-year-old lead her mom in the prayer of salvation! Her mom hugged her and said, 'Thank you, Jessica.'

"On the flip side of the soul-winning card, it is written in Spanish. Jessica's family speaks Spanish and English. Her mom said that she was going to work with Jessica on pronouncing the Spanish side so that she can minister to Spanish families when we hand out boxes of food on Saturdays! Glory to God!"

"Last Saturday afternoon, I was waiting at a bus stop in Washington, D.C., when two teenage girls joined me on the bench to also wait for the bus. I quickly thought to unleash the 'script' on them, and after shutting fear up, I proceeded. One of them claimed she had already asked Jesus into her heart, even though both confessed that they knew they would go to hell if they died that day. I asked the other girl if she had confessed Jesus as Lord. She said no. I asked if she wanted to, and she said yes! I led her in prayer out loud, and, praise God, she now belongs to Jesus.

"A few hours ago, I was at the grocery store shopping for food when an older gentleman stopped to ask if I had 25 cents to spare. I gave him 50 cents and asked him 'The Question.' After he said he wanted to be sure that he would be with Jesus forever, I asked him to repeat the prayer of salvation after me out loud. He repeated it so *loud*, right there in the aisle, and got saved. Praise God! I was so happy, and so was he. That was the best 50 cents I've ever spent! Hallelujah!"

"At a hotel on Saturday for a convention, I called the front desk for a refrigerator. We needed one because we had bought a lot of organic food for the week. They were all out of refrigerators because of another convention that was going on there. Jose brought an ice chest for us to use instead. I asked him if he went to church, and he said no. Then I asked him, 'Where would you go if you died tonight?' He said he didn't know. So I shared the scriptures in Romans with him. He accepted Jesus and then he said, 'The Lord sent you here for me! I was so sad before I came to your room! Now I feel good!' Praise God!"

"At the convention on Wednesday, I went to the store in the hotel to buy some mints. The cashier's name was Wilma. I said, 'Wilma, we are having a meeting over at the U.S. Cellular Arena. What would stop you from coming tonight?' She said, 'I have to go to the doctor. My knee is hurting me!' I told her I was a believer and the Bible says in Mark 16 that if we believe, we will lay hands on the sick, and they will recover. I asked her if I could pray for her, and she said yes! Then I prayed this simple prayer: 'Father, I thank You that You said in Your Word that if we believed, we would lay hands on the sick, and they would recover. So in the Name of

Jesus, I tell the pain in Wilma's knee to be gone! Amen!'
Then I told Wilma to 'work' her knee. She said she felt
a heat sensation in her knee and that the pain was gone!
Hallelujah!"

"As we were driving downtown, we passed Pancho's
Mexican Restaurant. Riley said, 'Let's stop there.' We
turned the bus around, and a few of us went in. Riley
walked up to the manager and asked if we could say a
prayer over the troops while everyone was eating. She
said, 'Sure!' Riley addressed the crowd, 'Hello, everyone, my name is Riley, and I am a minister at EMIC.
While you're eating, I'd like to say a quick prayer over
our troops.' Everyone in the restaurant bowed their
heads. Riley began, 'Lord, I thank You for protecting our
troops.... I thank You for these wonderful people here in
this restaurant.' Then he said, 'If anyone here does not
know beyond a shadow of a doubt that you would go to
heaven if you died tonight, repeat this prayer after me:
"Lord Jesus, come into my heart...."' Several people in
the restaurant prayed that prayer. We turned around to
face the manager and a few employees. Riley asked the
manager, 'Did you pray that prayer?' She said, 'Yes.' Then
he asked another employee, 'Did you pray that prayer?'
She said, 'Yes, and I don't normally pray prayers. But I
did this time!' Glory to God!

"When we got back on the bus, Allison said, 'Riley, as
we were waiting, we turned the bus around. As we did, I
saw a Bingo Hall at the end of the shopping center with
tons of people inside!' Riley said, 'Let's go!' We walked
into the Bingo Hall; there were at least 200 people in
there! Hallelujah! We had found a large fishing hole!

"Riley walked in and went up to the person in charge. As he was talking to her, a few of us were gathered around the door. An employee walked up to me and said, 'Do you want to buy a Bingo card for $1?' I said, 'No, thank you. We are here to pray a prayer for the troops.' She said, 'Oh, they will never let you do that!' As I spoke to her and shared the Word with her, she prayed the prayer to ask Jesus into her heart. Then she said, 'Maybe they'll let you pray!' She was changed!

"When that Bingo game was over, Riley got the microphone and said, 'Lord, I thank You for our troops that are protecting our country. And I thank You for these wonderful people....' Then he said, 'If you are not certain that you would go to heaven when you die, repeat this prayer after me: "Lord Jesus, come into my heart...."' If you have pain in your body, say: "Pain, go, in Jesus' Name. I am healed! Amen!" If you prayed that prayer to ask Jesus into your heart, raise your hand.' Hands went up all over the room! At least 65 people prayed with us for salvation! Glory!"

Thank you for taking the time to read this book. I truly believe if you will use the same principles I've outlined here, you will see a harvest of souls beyond your ability to count. In order to move in His power, we must *move!* The words of the Bible are just words to the world until we move out and show them Jesus.

You have God on the inside of you! The Father, the Son and the Holy Spirit dwell in your very being. Your DNA changed the day you became born again! You cannot fail! You can say with confidence, "Greater is He that is in me than he that is in the world!"

God is always with you! Do not let fear paralyze you any longer. God wants to use you today! You now have understanding from the Word of God and information in your hands! Go to my website and download the *Pocket Reference for Soul Winning* card. Start with your friends, family, neighbors and co-workers. Tell them, "I just read a book by this guy, and he gave me an assignment. Can you help me out? I have a few questions to ask!" You will never be the same.

Get ready for the greatest adventure and satisfaction of your life! I am praying for an abundant harvest in your life! I'm ready to hear, so email me with your testimonies.

Riley Stephenson
www.rileystephenson.com

Salvation
Scriptures

The fruit of the righteous is a tree of life; and he that winneth souls is wise (Proverbs 11:30).

And they that be wise shall shine as the brightness of the firmament; and they that turn many to righteousness as the stars for ever and ever (Daniel 12:3).

And he saith unto them, Follow me, and I will make you fishers of men (Matthew 4:19).

For though I be free from all men, yet have I made myself servant unto all, that I might gain the more. And unto the Jews I became as a Jew, that I might gain the Jews; to them that are under the law, as under the law, that I might gain them that are under the law (1 Corinthians 9:19-20).

And others save with fear, pulling them out of the fire (Jude 23).

Then saith he unto his disciples, The harvest truly is plenteous, but the labourers are few (Matthew 9:37).

But when the fruit is brought forth, immediately he putteth in the sickle, because the harvest is come (Mark 4:29).

Therefore said he unto them, The harvest truly is great, but the labourers are few: pray ye therefore the Lord of the harvest, the he would send forth labourers into his harvest (Luke 10:2).

Say not ye, There are yet four months, and then cometh havest? Behold, I say unto you, Lift up your eyes, and look on the fields; for they are white already to harvest (John 4:35).

And let us not be weary in well doing: for in due season we shall reap, if we faint not (Galatians 6:9).

Brethren, my heart's desire and prayer to God for Israel is, that they might be saved (Romans 10:1).

To the weak became I as weak, that I might gain the weak: I am made all things to all men, that I might by all means save some (1 Corinthians 9:22).

For whosoever shall give you a cup of water to drink in my name, because ye belong to Christ, verily I say unto you, he shall not lose his reward (Mark 9:41).

Therefore, my beloved brethren, be ye steadfast, unmoveable, always abounding in the work of the Lord, forasmuch as ye know that your labour is not in vain in the Lord (1 Corinthians 15:58).

For God is not unrighteous to forget your work and labour of love, which ye have shewed toward his name, in that ye have ministered to the saints, and do minister (Hebrews 6:10).

But whoso looketh into the perfect law of liberty, and continueth therein, he being not a forgetful hearer, but a doer of the work, this man shall be blessed in his deed (James 1:25).

Then will I teach transgressors thy ways; and sinners shall be converted unto thee (Psalm 51:13).

He that goeth forth and weepeth, bearing precious seed, shall doubtless come again with rejoicing, bringing his sheaves with him (Psalm 126:6).

And when he cometh home, he calleth together his friends and neighbours, saying unto them, Rejoice with me; for I have found my sheep which was lost. I say unto you, that likewise joy shall be in heaven over one sinner that repenteth, more than over ninety and nine just persons, which need no repentance (Luke 15:6-7).

So, being sent on their way by the church, they passed through Phoenicia and Samaria, describing the conversion of the Gentiles; and they caused great joy to all the brethren (Acts 15:3, *NKJV*).

About the Author

Riley Stephenson has shared the love of Jesus with thousands of people over the past decade. As Minister of Evangelism for Eagle Mountain International Church and Kenneth Copeland Ministries, his mission is three-fold: *win the lost; mobilize the Body of Christ;* and *bring in the harvest!*

Riley accomplishes this mission through instruction, training and raising teams who are then equipped to go into their world and bring in a harvest of souls into the Kingdom. Discipleship is the key to effective evangelism. Jesus said in Matthew 28, "Go...make disciples...and teach." Through training materials, tracts and personal witnessing tools, Riley will lead you into a journey where your confidence will build, souls will be won and Jesus will turn and say, "Well done thou good and faithful servant."

Riley and his wife, Kim, reside in Fort Worth, Texas, with their two daughters, Kiley and Katie Grace.

For additional resources or to schedule a ministry engagement, please contact:

Riley Stephenson
P.O. Box 327
Newark, TX 76071

www.rileystephenson.com

Additional Books by
Riley Stephenson

I Sent You to Reap

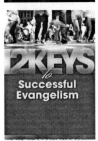

12 Keys to Successful Evangelism

Passion for Souls *(minibook)*

Go to kcm.org
Or call: **1-800-600-7395** (U.S. only)
+1-817-852-6000

When The LORD first spoke to Kenneth and Gloria Copeland about starting the *Believer's Voice of Victory* magazine...

He said: *This is your seed. Give it to everyone who ever responds to your ministry, and don't ever allow anyone to pay for a subscription!*

For nearly 40 years, it has been the joy of Kenneth Copeland Ministries to bring the good news to believers. Readers enjoy teaching from ministers who write from lives of living contact with God, and testimonies from believers experiencing victory through God's Word in their everyday lives.

Today, the *BVOV* magazine is mailed monthly, bringing encouragement and blessing to believers around the world. Many even use it as a ministry tool, passing it on to others who desire to know Jesus and grow in their faith!

Request your FREE subscription to the *Believer's Voice of Victory* magazine today!

Go to **freevictory.com** to subscribe online, or call us at **1-800-600-7395** (U.S. only) or **+1-817-852-6000**.

CPSIA information can be obtained at www.ICGtesting.com
Printed in the USA
LVOW10s0004021013

354709LV00004B/6/P